A STORY OF R

"E F F" FATHER'S DAY

*Overcoming challenges is
what makes life meaningful*

**MICHAEL M. WILKINS
MICHAEL L. WILKINS**

ISBN for the Print Book - ISBN: 978-1-7373580-0-8

ISBN for the Ebook - ISBN: 978-1-7373580-1-5

Printed by Lynk Press Publishing, Inc. in the United States of America

First Printing 2021.

www.mikelynkspeaks.com

DEDICATION

This book is dedicated to:

- anyone who has struggled with not having their biological father in their life
- the kid living inside the adult who yearns to know and have a healthy relationship with their father
- those who grew up without a father and was raised by their mother, grandparents, foster care, or legal guardian
- those who still struggle with the absence and have unanswered questions

When you grow up like this, the question that lingers is - *Dad, why weren't you an active participant in my life*?

- those who have allowed pride, lack of information and in some cases a secretive mother (who labeled their silence as protection) keep them from searching for the truth
- those who don't have the strength to take the first step to freedom
- the child who says to themselves - *Why should I do anything? I'm not the parent!*

Freedom from hurt, hatred, and bitterness is available to you. It's found in your decisions and what you decide to do next. You have a "CHOICE"!

This book is also dedicated to the Foundations of Faith Leadership Institute of Gethsemane Community Fellowship Baptist Church. It's in Foundations of Faith where I received wise counsel and submitted to a two-year curriculum that taught me how to be a better leader in every part of my life. As a participant, I expanded my education on leadership. With the help of my instructors I discovered some deep truths about myself. It's in this institution and those classrooms where I found the missing fragments of my identity. I faced my burdens head on, and by the grace of God I found forgiveness. I'm grateful for Foundations of Faith as it helped me become a better leader and take better control of my life.

Lastly, I dedicate this book to my now deceased father. Yes, the man who walked out on me and left his family homeless, abandoned, and fatherless for twenty-four years. Despite this, his truth inspired me to write this book, he was man enough to own his mistakes. His willingness to share his truth relieved my pain. His honesty about why he was absent taught me to find my once silent voice. His absence and choices pushed me to make different choices in my life. Although he was not in the home, for the time he was present I did learn some good things that I took into adulthood, but in large part I had to find other outlets to learn how to be a man. In these other role models, I learned to be respectful, kind, and generous. My father was a man I thought had no heart and no room to teach me anything but to the contrary it was he and God who taught me how to have a heart. In his absence I developed compassion for other fatherless people. My father is the co-author of this book because his penned answers to my questions many years ago, are included. He was always a writer, but he never became an author of his own book. I feel honored to have co-written this with him. Above everything that transpired in my childhood, what is most important to me is that I honor my father and mother, so that I may live long in the land of the LORD my God.

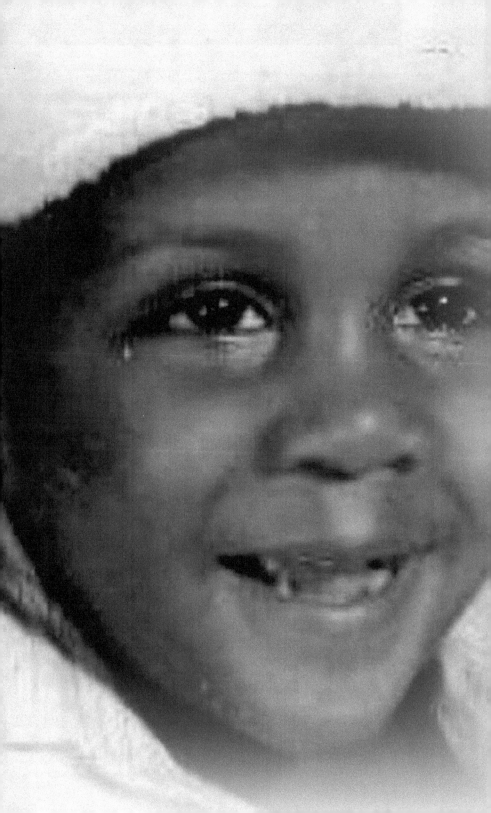

CONTENT

EARLY MEMORIES
IN THE BEGINNING

My parents were married when I was born, but their marriage ended before I became a teenager. I can recall several disagreements between them, and as a child, my mind was overwhelmed with more bad memories than fond ones. My father smoked, drank and abused drugs. I believe it was the combination of these things that made situations worse. I have two vivid memories of my father that were the source of my resentment towards him. I can recall an incident where my father hit my mom because she changed the channel on the television during a commercial break. The second memory was when my father came home under the influence. This time, he was slurring his words and he grabbed and hit my mother. One thing about my mom, she was not one to just stand there and take it. During this tussle, my father's shoe came off. When my mother got ahold of it, she used it to defend herself. She hit my father on his forehead and it split his head open above his eyebrow and it started bleeding. She also grabbed a broom and broke it over her thigh because she was prepared to keep defending herself, If the fight had escalated any further. I believe my mother would have stabbed him with that broken broom and my story might have taken a different turn. That was my mom's last straw. In some way, I think she might have knocked him sober with the shoe because he decided not to fight back and he left the house.

That was the last time my father put his hands on my mom. I was about 12 years old at the time, and I have no recollection of my father living with us after that. The downfall of our family was that my father spent his money on drugs and alcohol instead of taking care of us. Shortly after his disappearance and one afternoon after school, I got off the school bus and saw our furniture on the lawn. In the neighborhood I grew up in, this meant we were being kicked out of our home. I realized shortly after that we were going to be homeless. I was so embarrassed that I took off running.

Self-Reflection
Early Memories

"Finally, brothers, whatever is true, whatever is honorable, whatever is just, whatever is pure, whatever is lovely, whatever is commendable, if there is any excellence, if there is anything worthy of praise, think about these things." (ESV, Philippians 4:8)

Reflection Question

What information do you have about your absent parent?

_____

_____

_____

_____

_____

_____

_____

_____

_____

"The worst part of holding the memories is not the pain. It's the loneliness of it. Memories need to be shared."

~ Author: Lois Lowry

HARDENED HEART
THE FEELINGS

Angry, Confused, Embarrassed. Deeply Hurt! I had so many emotions the day I got off that bus. I mainly felt embarrassed as my friends watched us get kicked out.

Despite the rocky times we had with my father, he was the one I was looking for that day. He was nowhere to be found and he did not come to our rescue. From what I could tell, my father abandoned us, and I ran far away from that place I called home. I wanted to hide. I stayed away from the house for some time and eventually my sister found me. My father's absence was a punch in the gut.

I already had feelings of hate toward my dad and ending up on the street cemented those feelings. My heart began to harden towards him. My father was out of sight and for that I put him out of my mind. As the years passed, the relationship soured. I put any love I had for him in a grave. Homelessness felt uncertain, lonely, cold, and scary. In my mind he was the cause and I hated how it made me feel. I often wondered about the impact it had on my mother and sister.

That time in my life was rough but it was a turning point for me at the same time. I vowed to be nothing like my father in any way, shape, or form. Growing up I heard that men were supposed to protect and provide for their families. My experience was the exact opposite. I felt the most unprotected, when I could not find my Dad that day and his lack of provision had us living in my mom's car.

Self-Reflection
Hardened Heart

"Come to me, all who labor and are heavy laden, and I will give you rest." (ESV, Matthew 11:28)

Reflection Question

Describe your specific feelings toward your absent parent.

_____

_____

_____

_____

_____

_____

_____

_____

_____

_____

_____

_____

"It's the hard things that break; soft things don't break. It was an epiphany I had today and I just wonder why it took me so very, very long to see it! You can waste so many years of your life trying to become something hard in order not to break; but it's the soft things that can't break! The hard things are the ones that shatter into a million pieces!"

~ Author: C. JoyBell C.

SEPARATED

TIME AND DISTANCE

Over the years, my father reached out a handful of times to make contact and rebuild our relationship. I rarely talked to him. Quite frankly, I wanted nothing to do with him. I would often think, *'What kind of man would do this to his family?'* I always wanted a positive male role model, and for that, I started watching fathers in other families almost everywhere I went. I often thought how lucky those kids were to have their dad's support. Mine was not there to witness anything I did as a teenager. There is one exception, high school graduation. On graduation day, the venue reached max capacity quickly, which unfortunately meant that many ticketed guests had to stay outside. When the ceremony was over, I learned that my father made it inside and my mother did not. That seemed so unfair. When I saw him outside, he congratulated me, but I ignored him. I was more concerned about why my mom didn't make it in and upset that she could not watch me cross the stage. This was a big deal for us because my mom did not get a chance to finish high school and seeing me graduate would have been special. I had no words for my father that day, I left with my mother and other family members and went on with my life.

My father and I remained estranged after high school. I've always known where he lived, and I also knew that he would inquire about us from time to time. I did not care that he was asking, I completely shut him out. After high school, I was confused about what a man was supposed to be or do in this world. I was lost. My mom pushed for me to take the next step in life by giving me an ultimatum to either go to college or the military. I chose college and graduated from Norfolk State University.

While in college, I joined Alpha Phi Alpha Fraternity, Inc. In the fraternity, I found several positive male role models. I had several brothers, but God placed one brother in my life whose walk with Christ I admired. He invited me to church, and I was grateful because I hadn't attended in a long time. My goal was to rekindle my relationship with the Lord, and I did. While in church, two things started happening:

1) I started forgiving myself for burdens I chose to carry very early on in my life and 2) I started questioning if my father deserved forgiveness.

Relevant Verses:

"Be kind to one another, tenderhearted, forgiving one another, as God in Christ forgave you."
(ESV, Ephesians 4:32)

"But if you do not forgive others their trespasses, neither will your Father forgive your trespasses."
(ESV, Matthew 6:15)

"And when you stand praying, forgive, if you hold anything against anyone, forgive them, so that your Father in heaven may forgive you your sins."
(NIV, Mark 11:25)

Self-Reflection
Separated

"Draw near to God, and he will draw near to you..."
(ESV, James 4:8)

Reflection Question

What questions have surfaced for you throughout your life about your absent parent?

_____

_____

_____

_____

_____

_____

_____

_____

_____

_____

SEVEN WAYS I FOUND THE PATH TO FORGIVENESS

ACKNOWLEDGE

Growing up, I was left with negative thoughts and un-answered questions. My father was not around to fill in the blanks, my mom had to work, and my older sister was in her own world and had her own issues with our father. I felt like I had to fend for myself. After all that I experienced, I felt hurt. For example, at my football or basketball games and other events, seeing fathers with their children was a constant reminder of the sup-port I did not receive. In junior high school, these feel-ings turned into bad behavior. I got into a few fights and this had a negative impact on my mother. I know now that my behavior was completely connected to my father's absence. Ultimately, one thing I realized is that I did not want to disappoint my mom. I knew right from wrong and I started to wonder which way my life was headed. I realized I was not in a good mental space and I knew something had to change.

To acknowledge how I felt, I spent time reliving the first few months of my father's absence. I sat with my-self and dug up every bit of hurt, pain and disappoint-ment I was feeling. I assessed each thing that came to mind and was wondering if I wanted to confront my fa-ther with the memories that kept resurfacing. I second guessed myself all the time, I thought *'Do I have the courage to ask all of these questions?'*. I know now that I had no confidence to ask them any sooner than I did. I avoided it for a long time. I feared confronting the pain I carried. I told myself, *'Everything is alright',* *'Everything is fine',* or *'I'll be good by myself'*. Although the feelings were hard to navigate, I did not want to give up on finding answers.

Acknowledgment was the beginning of the healing process for me.

Self-Reflection
Acknowledge

"Trust in the Lord with all your heart and lean not on your own understanding;" (NIV, Proverbs 3:5)

Reflection Question

What do you need to acknowledge?

_____

_____

_____

_____

_____

_____

_____

_____

_____

_____

_____

_____

When we acknowledge a child's feelings, we do
him a great service. We put him in touch with
his inner reality. And once he's clear about that
reality, he gathers the strength
to begin to cope."

~ Author: Adele Faber

COMMIT YOUR WAY

I was committed to going through a process that would help me release the burdens of my past. That included committing to acknowledging how I felt and taking many more positive steps towards what would set me free from feeling so heavy. I often went into deep thought about why I didn't know my father as a person and why he wasn't around. It was easy to suppress my feelings, but I didn't want my circumstance to control me. After acknowledging how I felt, I didn't want to abandon the process. I made a commitment to myself that I wanted to honor. Keeping my word to myself was important. There was no turning back for me, I was going to take control of the person I was becoming and commit to moving forward.

While going through this process, there was something subconscious that was being uncovered. It wasn't until I started either talking or writing about my feelings, that I realized what I was holding onto. Although it was painful, I kept unpacking everything stored in my mind. Figuring out how I could rid myself of the emotional baggage surrounding my father's absence was important, especially prior to any kind of reconciliation. To be honest, I did not know if reconciliation was possible, but I no longer wanted to suppress what I felt. The truth is I felt incomplete as a person. There was a burden I was carrying, and I was ready to put it down.

Over the years, I spent time asking myself questions and made very little progress finding answers. I would wonder, *'How do I fix it?'* Not them, but me. I decided, professional help was a part of my plan. This can be a difficult process to navigate on your own. I started down a path to resolve the feelings of pain, hurt and bitterness, I wanted to replace those feelings with joy, peace, and love. Getting to that place was my responsibility. I wanted to heal, and I longed for wholeness. I was committing to a different way of being.

Boys and men are taught to suppress emotions, but I didn't want to carry on like that. Emotional wholeness is the idea that every human being has a whole emotional make-up that is operating in every moment in time. This means that in every moment of our lives, at the same time, we are happy and sad, confident and afraid, loving and angry, comfortable and uncomfortable, and so forth.[1] A man must find a healthy balance within his emotions and finding that balance was my goal.

I committed myself to sifting through things I tried to forget. Over time, I buried memories of bits and pieces of my life. I spent time examining the negative feelings I held onto to understand if they were the reason my life seemed to have so many missing pieces.

Relevant Verse:

"The LORD is close to the brokenhearted and saves those who are crushed in spirit". (NIV, Psalm 34:18)

---

1   https://medium.com/emovera-founder-blog/emotional-wholeness-148437834afe

Self-Reflection
Commit Your Way

"Commit everything you do to the LORD. Trust him, and he will help you." (NLT, Psalm 37:5)

Reflection Question

What is your plan to reap the benefits of committing to this process?

_____

_____

_____

_____

_____

_____

_____

_____

_____

_____

_____

"When confronted with a challenge, the committed heart will search for a solution. The undecided heart searches for an escape."

~ Author: Andy Andrews

SEEK WISE COUNSEL

My family is Christian, and although there was a period in my teens where I stopped going to church, I still knew I wanted spiritual counsel. As I mentioned, a fraternity brother re-introduced me to church during college, and because of that I recommitted myself to going regularly.

Before confronting my father, reconciliation with myself was the priority. During this healing process, there were constant reminders of the fact that my father was not in my life. I was triggered repeatedly by certain sermons and experiences in church. These weren't bad experiences, just reminders of his absence. As I was letting God in, the Word (Holy Bible) was shedding light on areas of my heart that were broken.

At my church, I entered a two-year personal development program called Foundations of Faith Leadership Institute. The program provided counseling, structure, and critical thinking. I was drawn to the program because of its focus on leadership. What I wanted more than anything was to be a good leader. It helped me to think about how I wanted to reshape my life and create a new legacy for myself and my future family.

Based on what I knew, I was excited about the program but unexpectedly, it shed light on the importance of emotional, spiritual, and mental health. There were several exercises that helped to soften my heart and forced me to address some buried feelings. I was able to release anger, bitterness, and hatred. I never thought a program about leadership would prompt me to confront some of my most troubling issues. While completing the program, I did not want to revisit old, painful memories. As a child, I pushed things down so deep and put a band-aid on a wound that required a much larger covering.

Things did not change overnight; it was a long process. Ultimately, the program helped me to become a better leader at school, work, in ministry and in life. It did not stop there because I was also being drawn to take the lead in restoring a relationship with my father.

Seeking wise counsel was an integral part of my process. I wanted to move forward with a new and clear mind. I no longer wanted to ignore what I was feeling because ignoring it didn't feel like progress. Professional support helped me to gain new perspective about what happened in my past. I got the chance to walk alongside others whose objective was to see me do better. At the end of the road, a healthy well-being and mind set was the goal.

Relevant Verses:

"Your word is a lamp to my feet and a light to my path."
(ESV, Psalm 119:105)

"I will instruct you and teach you in the way you should go; I will counsel you with my loving eye on you."
(NIV, Psalm 32:8)

Self-Reflection
Seek Wise Counsel

"Without counsel plans fail, but with many advisers they succeed." *(ESV, Proverbs 15:22)*

Reflection Question

How do you think wise counsel can help you in this process?

_____

_____

_____

_____

_____

_____

_____

_____

_____

_____

"There are moments in our lives when we summon the courage to make choices that go against reason, against common sense and the wise counsel of people we trust. But we lean forward nonetheless because, despite all risks and rational arguments, we believe that the path we are choosing is right and best thing to do. We refuse to be bystanders, even if we do not know exactly where our actions will lead."

~ Author: Howard Schultz

FIND YOUR VOICE.

BE FEARLESS. MAKE A DIFFERENCE.

GET INSPIRED.

HAVE HEART. DO THE RIGHT THING.

SURROUND YOURSELF WITH GOOD FRIENDS.

TAKE CHANCES. ASK QUESTIONS.

FOLLOW YOUR DREAMS.

DISCOVER YOUR PASSION.

LEARN SOMETHING NEW EVERY DAY.

BE KIND AND GENEROUS.

LIVE YOUR LIFE WITH ABANDON.

MAKE A DIFFERENCE.

THIS IS YOUR TIME.

MAKE IT PLAIN

rite it out and make it plain. This step could be in-
terchangeable with the previous step – seek wise
counsel, simply because it can be hard to open up to
someone without first acknowledging how you feel.

I received a journal as a gift over 20+ years ago and
on the cover, it had inspiring phrases like 'find your
voice', be fearless', 'do the right thing', 'take chances'
and 'have heart'. I was inspired by those phrases and
one day while looking through old things, I came across
the journal and when I read those phrases again, the
Holy Spirit clearly instructed me to start jotting down
my unanswered questions. Each question flowed out
of me with ease. I was clear on what I wanted to know.

Since I spent many years without my father, I had
to dig through quite a bit of 'stuff'. It was like taking
a machete to tall weeds in the jungle. There was so
much to plow through. I spent quite a bit of time, writing down every question I could think of. My approach
was to write as if I was standing face to face with my father. I wrote questions about the hurt and pain. Writing
became a substitute for confronting the father that was

not there. I wrote every thought and 'said' everything I had to say in the book.

The process was therapeutic It felt like a big weight was lifted. After dedicating time to getting it out, I knew I didn't have to carry it anymore. I wrote it down and made it plain and it was a relief.

This is what I wrote:

Pops please take the time to answer these questions because it is really important to me. I have a lot to learn from you because over the years I've created my own perception of who you are from what I've known from childhood up to this point as an adult. I have to be honest with you, my perception of you reeks with hatred. Despite these feelings I want to make up for lost time. I need you to be honest and don't sugar coat any of your answers. If you find that you can't answer all the questions in their entirety, then this will be the only attempt from me and the only opportunity for you to make things right between us. When you are finished with the questions call me and I'll come pick up the book.

I love you....

These are some of the questions I jotted down.

- *Pops when you were a kid what was your relationship like with your father?*

- *Pops what knowledge did you gain from watching your dad be a father?*

- *Pops what type of values did your father teach you?*

- *Pops did you learn from your parents growing up?*

- *Pops how did those lessons shape your thoughts on what type of man, husband, and father you wanted to become?*
- *Pops when you became a husband to my mother how would you describe the type of man you were at that time?*
- *Pops how did drinking and doing drugs impact your life? Pops what drugs did you use?*
- *Pops give me a list of things you did that you would consider irresponsible that you have done as man?*
- *Pops what was the hardest things you had to deal with mentally about my sister and I after you and my mother separated?*
- *Pops did you cheat on my mother?*
- *Pops if you could go back in time what would you change about yourself?*
- *Pops what would you change about our relationship?*

Relevant Verses:

"Create in me a clean heart, O God, and renew a right spirit within me." (ESV, Psalm 51:10)

"Peace I leave with you; my peace I give you. I do not give to you as the world gives. Do not let your hearts be troubled, and do not be afraid." (NIV, John 14:27)

Self-Reflection
Make it Plain

"And the Lord answered me: Write the vision; make it plain on tablets, so he may run who reads it."
(ESV, Habakkuk 2:2)

Reflection Question

Write out the questions you would ask your absent parent.

_____

_____

_____

_____

_____

_____

_____

_____

_____

_____

SEEK THE TRUTH

THIS IS HARD! I think we can agree that when you begin to look for answers, there is fear about what you might find. When thinking about who should be questioned, my mom came to mind. I wasn't sure if I wanted to confront my mom or leave her out of this. My initial thoughts were that my mom was there for me and she had gone through enough with my father. I did not want to drudge up any buried feelings she might have by confronting her with my questions. I shared in the pain she experienced. I loved my mom so much that I did not want to approach her, but I came to the conclusion that for true healing, it was important to confront both parents.

I confronted my parents, and here's where 'leaning not on your own understanding' comes into play. Many of you may have heard the popular acronym for FEAR: *False Evidence Appearing Real,* and because of my fear I made up several stories as to the reason why things happened the way they did. When I wasn't confronting the source of my pain, I created a false reality that lacked evidence to support my thoughts. I wanted to seek the truth because it was important to know if the stories I created in my head were real. I created reasons as to why my father did not put forth better effort to be a responsible husband and supportive father. When I was in my own head about what happened in the past, I was also in poor mental health. I knew that regardless of what I thought I knew, there were two people who knew the truth.

My mother's visceral reaction to anything having to do with my father is what made it hard for me to confront her about why my father did what he did. If my father's name was mentioned, my mother's negative facial expressions and rolling eyes were enough to let me know that she hated my father. To this day, my mother will not call me by my first name because it reminds her of my father. Despite his actions, bad behavior and the pain he caused, over the years, my mom has never spoken poorly of my father to me or my sister.

I did not know if she would get past her anger so that I could get the truth, but I had to start with her. I confronted my mother and talked to her about everything I saw, including the arguments, domestic violence, unhappiness, and disagreements. We talked about how their relationship crumbled before my eyes. Her advice to me in these conversations was, *'Never tolerate abuse or be abusive to others in your relationships'*. My mom only had some of the answers and she advised that I go to my father to get the rest of them. Before meeting with my father, I spent time meditating and praying about my next steps. When I finally met with him, I gave him the journal, with the phrases on the cover, where I had written my questions. Again, I've always known where my father lived, so I took my book to him and told him to read it. With that, I also said: *'You know we don't have a relationship because you chose* to remain absent for the better part of my life. Life feels incomplete because of your absence. It helped create this hurt and emptiness inside of me and I need to know the truth. If I can't get the truth, then I don't know how to explain what is going on, on the inside, or where it is going to take me in life. If I cannot get answers from you, then this will be my last time talking to you. I'm asking you to take this book, open it, read what's in it and answer every single question truthfully and please don't sugar coat it. When you're finished with it, call me and I will come and get the book.' My father took the book.

The following pages are my Dad's handwritten answers to my questions.

My dearest beloved son,

I guess you can say that I fell in love with your mother at first sight. Back there then she was the most beautiful woman in the whole world to me. She had the most perfect figure and when I first looked into her eyes, I believed she had most been heavenly sent. She once meant the whole world too me.

I told her what I wanted in life and at the time, she said that she wanted the same things too. I ~~married~~ proposed to your mother when she was four months pregnant with your sister. I remember it very clearly it was on my mother's sister birthday Dee. 22, 1973 three days before Christmas and nine days before her birthday, which was on Dee. 31, 1973.

I married her on my twenty first

birthday, Feb. 9, 1974. I remember that
I had called my father and he said ask me
this question. You can't wait until you're grown
to get married and why so young.

I explained to him that your
mother was pregnant with Nikki Nikie
and I wanted to the right thing by her.
I didn't want my daughter to be born out
of weddlock. To me marriage was the most
honorable thing to do and besides I didn't
want my child to go thrugh the same things
I went through. Not knowing and being so confused
until I was old enough to understand and chose
to believe.

Now even though I took care of the
family first, the money I had left, I and your undeles,
Douglas, Gregory, and Isage would go out clubing
all the time. I smoked and snorted coke I
smoked weed, and was poping pills, like angel dust,

son, and I'm so sorry, way deep down in my soul,
to the ~~very heart~~ it cut through my very heart

I can't make up for lost time,
but I hope and pray my writing these words,
that they will draw us closer together. May
God bless you and keep you all the days of
your life, and peace onto you, my beloved son.

P.S. I have already ~~answered~~
answered what kind of drugs I used in question
number six. (6) Please don't get caught up
doing drugs like I did, trying to get higher and
higher. Always remember, I really mean always
The first high that you take, can't make you
get any higher. For the love of God don't
put any needles into your arms, I never
did. (This Is Called Shooting Up) Drugs Can
kill!!!

~~My dearest beloveds~~ My dearest and most beloved ~~son~~, cloning drugs in my life have effected me in a very strange kind of way. It took me away from you and family. Mostly you beause I wasn't quite there to show ~~and teach~~ you how to ~~become a man~~ As you know alebhol is a drug too and I wasn't there for you doing your teenage years. I wasn't quite there to guide you on your way.

I regret having not being close too you in the past, not being able to tell you how, and why your mother and I had t be separated and ~~divorce~~ divorce. Mainly it was drugs and partying. It separated ~~f~~ me from my family. This is why you are asking me these kind of questions now. I woudn't be suprise if you have even more for me to answer. I deeply regret all of it my dearest

Today I can say, that through God's help I drink once and awhile, do not take drugs, only doctor's medication that prescribe for me. I've learned how to ~~repect~~ respect myself as well as others. I've learned to respect my immedately family and life as well. I ~~have~~ a much more better look on life and ~~have~~ think of my future with my entie family.

I now take life one day at a time, travel, love of family ~~so~~ much more, love of God and Church. I have learned so much more love and ~~respet~~ respect for my family and friends, and neighbors alike,

I've learned to love you ~~my~~ dearest beloved son, and your sister, so much deeper then I ever before.

(6) My dearly beloved son, If I could
go back in time, I wouldn't certainly ~~be that~~ not live that
kind of life. I would have loved you all ~~much~~ so
much better. I ~~had~~ would have respected you all
so much better. Most of all I would have
respected myself, after all how can you
love and respect somebody, if you don't have
love and respect for yourself. I was kind of
a selfish man then. I would consider ~~other~~
people's feelings. ~~Mostly all~~ Most of all my
family. I wouldn't have gone out and party so
much and would have spend more time with your
mother, sister, and ~~your~~ First of all I would
have been more delicated to God and my church
You see If I had put God first and most of
all, I could have taken care you all so much
better. You see "God Is Love," for He gave His
only begotten Son, that toe would not perish, but have
forever lasting life."

what I used to look like. I was ashamed and couldn't hold my head up high that night, but we walked on to the mall and dinner.

I secretly threw all the drugs out of the house and silently cried that night.

I prayed to God to take the taste of drugs away from me. Son, I was so young and I had to spread my wild oaks. I hadn't fully matured. Don't hate me for this, please don't hold against me, I'm sorry, so sorry that I didn't show you the type of love and affection back then.

You're young still but please don't make the same mistakes I had in the past. So far I've seen the better man in you and I'm so very, very proud of you. You're taking your time to start a family, just be sure you're completely delicated to the woman you're marrying and your children if you decide to have any. (I hope you do, before I die

window pane, acid, anything I could get my hands on.
I throught to myself, I was doing it as an
experiment so I could tell my children not to do
drugs or drink. My biggest down fall was smoking
rack cocaine, I was going down hill fast and I
moved back to Suffolk, after your mother and I separated
separated,

Thanks to your sister, I finally quick
aking drugs, but I contiune drinking until I had
my frst stroke. I'm so sorry that I took you,
your mother, and sister thraugh that pain and
misery. It was a fad for my generation and
everybody was doing it. You see I went to give
your sister and she snacthed away from me, she
said that she could see the devil in me and
I quick cold turkey that night. We was walking
one day, and I was taking you out for dinner to Tower
Mall, your uncles and Isaac, was standing
on someone's porch amd your sister told me that's

Self-Reflection
Seek the Truth

"Then you will know the truth, and the truth will set you free." (NIV, John 8:32)

Reflection Question

What are you holding onto that you need to put behind you? What are some examples where you've exercised forgiveness?

_____

_____

_____

_____

_____

_____

_____

_____

_____

_____

"We awaken by asking the right questions. We awaken when we see knowledge being spread that goes against our own personal experiences. We awaken when we see popular opinion being wrong but accepted as being right, and what is right being pushed as being wrong. We awaken by seeking answers in corners that are not popular. And we awaken by turning on the light inside when everything outside feels dark."

~ Author: Suzy Kassem

GET UNDERSTANDING

My father returned the book to me with answers. Even after getting answers, getting understanding of everything I now knew was a critical part of the process to reconciliation.

My objective was to get clear on the 'why' questions so that I could move past those feelings of being unwanted. Through his answers, I learned what was going on with him during that period of his life. I even found that I had some misinformation. Although I was happy I had answers, some of them confirmed the painful thoughts I had. He chose drugs, alcohol and whatever he was doing in the streets over his family. I took in what my father had to say. I analyzed it, read it and re-read it and some of what I learned helped me to leave those old thoughts behind. It was also through wise counsel that I learned I could separate the person from their problems. This approach gave me a new perspective on my father. With concrete facts, I could make a conscious, more informed choice about how to move forward with our relationship. Confronting both parents was the best thing I could have done.

Before starting this process, the best I could hope for was that the answered questions and new information would close the hole in my heart, and it did. I was able to get the truth behind the stories that I created over the years. I could now turn the page and write a new story where the ending would be entirely up to me.

Relevant Verse:

"Wisdom is the principal thing; therefore get wisdom: and with all thy getting get understanding."
(KJV, Proverbs 4:7)

Self-Reflection
Get Understanding

"The beginning of wisdom is this: Get wisdom. Though it cost all you have, get understanding."
(NIV, Proverbs 4:7)

Reflection Question

What are the top 5 things you want to understand about why your parent was absent?

_____

_____

_____

_____

_____

_____

_____

_____

_____

_____

"Understanding comes through communication,
and through understanding we find
the way to peace."

~ Author: Ralph C. Smedley

GIVE GRACE

After seeking the truth and getting understanding, I was met with a choice on how I wanted to continue on in my life. What was I going to make 'moving forward' about? Who really needed to be released from the burdens of the past? My absent father? or myself? This step was about giving grace to myself, so that the relationship with my father could heal and grow. Once I realized that, I started to focus on my feelings, mental health, joy, and personal progress. With my new outlook, I felt I could begin to extend grace to my father, despite his absence.

On one hand, I could allow what I thought all those years to control me or I could become the leader in my own life and lead by example. I had to put some things aside including what I endured mentally and emotionally and forgive myself for the hardened heart that I developed and the bitterness I harbored. I had to own the fact that my negative thoughts contributed to my low self-worth and lack of enthusiasm for my life. When I look back at it, I behaved poorly and created mental and emotional problems for myself.

As early as the 9th grade and again in college, I asked myself *'Am I going to let these issues control me, or is Michael Markee Wilkins going to take control?'* I had to separate myself from the problems and issues that came from the absence of my father. But that was only part one, I also needed to forgive my father for some of the same reasons I needed to forgive myself. God did not create either of us to dishonor him or ourselves.

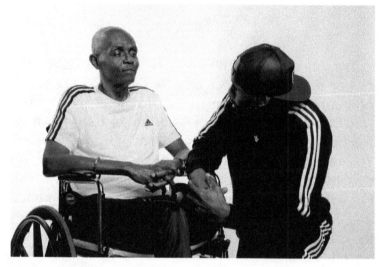

Even if you are not a believer (in Jesus Christ), I do not believe I or anybody was brought into this world to bring pain to other people, give off bad energy or be a negative person in general. Behaviors are learned and they can be unlearned. I believed I was a good leader, giver of good vibes, a good role model and a forgiving person. I chose to become a person filled with joy and happiness. In short, I decided to change.

Forgiveness and reconciliation is the name of the game in this step. I had forgiven myself but to forgive my father I had to separate the person from the decisions and problems that manifested. What I realized through this process was that God did not create my father to be an alcoholic, drug abuser, physically abusive to others or a bad father. My dad's choices contributed to what he became and as his son, I felt the brunt of those poor choices. What I learned was, it was okay for me to be angry at the drugs and alcohol, but not necessarily at my father, Michael Lindsey Wilkins. He was not created to be who he became and once I understood that, I was more upset with the choices than the human being.

Relevant Verses:

"Be kind to one another, tenderhearted, forgiving one another, as God in Christ forgave you."
(NIV, Ephesians 4:32)

"Cast all your anxiety on him because he cares for you." (NIV, 1 Peter 5:7)

Self-Reflection
Give Grace

"Be kind to one another, tenderhearted, forgiving one another, as God in Christ forgave you."
(ESV, Ephesians 4:32)

Reflection Question

What are you holding onto that you need to put behind you? What are some examples where you have exercised forgiveness? With whom do you need to reconcile?

_____

_____

_____

_____

_____

_____

_____

_____

_____

_____

FINALLY
MY HOPE FOR YOU...

My hope for you is that you would be courageous. I had so many emotions through my journey and so might you. Take a chance on yourself and pursue healing. This book is just a glimpse into a longer process of reconciliation. From what I've shared, I hope you feel courageous enough to take similar steps to learn more about the story of your absent parent. I hope that within these pages you find hope for what might be possible in your life. Each of us can lead ourselves out of the place where we have felt trapped by circumstances that were outside of our control.

My greatest wish for children who grew up with an absent father like me, is that you would find a life that is whole, peaceful, and free of confusion. Thank you for your interest in my journey and I hope you take your own steps towards healing and reconciliation.

Be courageous in these things:

- Acknowledge the emotions that come with having an absent parent
- Seek out your absent parent or relatives that can shed light on your story and ask the questions that you've always wanted to ask

- Allow others you trust to walk beside you and provide counsel that reshapes your perspective

Relevant Verses:

"Be strong and courageous. Do not fear or be in dread of them, for it is the Lord your God who goes with you. He will not leave you or forsake you." (ESV, Deuteronomy 31:6)

Self-Reflection
Finally

"May the God of hope fill you with all joy and peace in believing, so that by the power of the Holy Spirit you may abound in hope." (ESV, Romans 15:13)

Reflection Question

What is your HOPE for yourself and your FUTURE?

_____

_____

_____

_____

_____

_____

_____

_____

_____

_____

_____

"Honor your father and your mother, so that you may live long in the land the Lord your God is giving you." (NIV, Exodus 20:12)